AF255804

Tertullian Treatises

Concerning Prayer, Concerning Baptism

Tertullian's Treatises

Concerning Prayer, Concerning Baptism

Translated By

Alexander Souter

WIPF & STOCK · Eugene, Oregon

Wipf and Stock Publishers
199 W 8th Ave, Suite 3
Eugene, OR 97401

Tertullian's Treatises:
Concerning Prayer, Concerning Baptism
By Souter, Alexander
Softcover ISBN-13: 978-1-6667-6474-1
Hardcover ISBN-13: 978-1-6667-6475-8
eBook ISBN-13: 978-1-6667-6476-5
Publication date 11/10/2022
Previously published by SPCK, 1919

TO

THE HONOURED MEMORY

OF MY FATHER

ALEXANDER SOUTER

(1846–1918)

ALL HIS LIFE

AN ARDENT STUDENT

OF SACRED LITERATURE

PREFACE

Having been honoured with an invitation to contribute a translation of a portion of some Father's works, with the suggestion that Tertullian would be acceptable, I chose the sister treatises on Prayer and Baptism, in the belief that these would prove of as much interest as any to the constituency the S.P.C.K. seeks to reach. I cannot claim any special familiarity with these treatises, though I hope this volume may contain something of interest even to the professional scholar.

The introduction provides such matter as a Latin scholar who is not a theologian might be expected to contribute, with references to literature where the subject can be further studied. The translation has been made without the slightest reference to any preceding version, and must commend itself, or the reverse, by its own qualities. I have submitted it to the rigorous taste of my friend Mr. James Taylor, of the Aberdeen Centre for the Training of Teachers, and am conscious that it has profited exceedingly by his criticisms, for which I offer him my heartiest thanks. The Biblical references are given with a greater fullness than has been hitherto attempted. The notes, such as they are, depend hardly at all on any edition: no attempt has been made to repeat what will be found in the editions. The text

used as the basis of the translation is for the most part
that of Reifferscheid and Wissowa in the Vienna *Corpus
Scriptorum Ecclesiasticorum Latinorum*, Vgl. XX. (1890).
In it the scanty critical material at the disposal of the
editors has been used with judgment.

It is intended to publish other treatises of Tertullian
in this series.

The University, Aberdeen.
August 10, 1918.

INTRODUCTION

OF Tertullian, as of many another who has rendered pre-eminent service to humanity, almost nothing is known. His full name was Quintus Septimius Florens Tertullianus, and he was a native of the Roman province of Africa, which corresponded roughly in area to the modern Tunis. He was of pagan parentage, and underwent a complete training as a lawyer. He appears to have visited Italy, but he spent the greatest part of his life in the city of Carthage, which had been refounded by Julius Cæsar about a hundred years after the younger Scipio had laid it waste. The city had become once again a great centre, and Christianity must have reached it at an early period, probably direct from Italy. In Africa the new religion found a favourable soil, a fact not altogether undue to the Semitic origin of the old Punic stock, which found something akin to itself in the daughter of Judaism. The number of churches in Africa in Tertullian's time probably greatly exceeded the total of Italy itself. And this Christianity seems to have been more Latin than Greek. The most highly educated of the provincials in Africa were acquainted with Greek, but the proportion of such persons was far less than would have been found in Italy.

We have no evidence as to the date of Tertullian's

birth, but if we place it about A.D. 160 we shall probably not be far wrong. The date of his conversion is equally unknown, but it may be assigned to the period of mature manhood. He was a man of ardent temperament, unbounded energy and great creative faculty. In such a man conversion was sure to be followed at the earliest possible interval by active work on behalf of the Faith, and for him the pen was the obvious instrument. All his knowledge of law, literature and philosophy was at once enlisted on the side of the persecuted religion. Like a later convert from paganism, St. Ambrose, he must have taken up the study of the Scriptures as eagerly as he had followed his earlier pursuits. We have no satisfactory evidence that he held any office in the Church. It is safest to regard him as an early forerunner of a succession of Christian laymen, men like Pelagius, Marius Mercator, Junilius and Cassiodorus, who have had their share in building up the body of Christian doctrine.

The strongly ascetic vein in Tertullian led him later to adopt the doctrines of the Montanists. This sect took its name from Montanus of Pepuza in Phrygia, and among its tenets was the assertion of prophetic gifts in opposition to the regularly constituted ministry; millenarism, and abstinence from every sort of union between the sexes. The influence of Montanism spread gradually in the West, and reached Africa almost certainly from Italy, but it is improbable that it had become associated with a declared sect in Africa in Tertullian's time. It represented rather a tendency within the bosom of the Church. But that tendency gained more and more power with Tertullian himself, and in his later works he accepts the doctrine of the new prophecy, and inaugurates the arbitrary rule of individual spiritual gifts, thus undermining the authority of the Old and New Testaments as well as that of the Church. He contradicts Scripture in urging the Christian to face persecution, in depreciating marriage, in making regulations for fasting, and other minor matters.

But these and other exaggerations, though they have deprived Tertullian of canonisation, in no way affect his importance as the earliest of the Latin Fathers. His great learning, his obvious sincerity and his burning eloquence are to be set over against such excesses, as well as against the occasional coarseness which will break out in the writings of a Tertullian, a Jerome and an Augustine, who have in their unregenerate days become too familiar with uncleanness. In originality he is inferior to none of these. In doctrine and in language alike he is a pioneer of Western Christianity. To him we owe the first formulation of the doctrine of the Trinity ; to him we owe a great part of the Christian Latin vocabulary. He is the earliest Latin writer to quote Scripture with any freedom, and he is the first of that roll of noble names, Tertullian, Cyprian, Hilary, Ambrose, Jerome, Augustine, which no Christian literature in any language can match.

Yet here, also, we have our treasure in earthen vessels. Tertullian is the most difficult of all Latin prose writers, outdoing the fully developed Tacitean style in that brevity which inevitably becomes obscurity. His vocabulary is curiously compounded of technical legal language, Grecisms and colloquialisms, and in the absence of a special lexicon or a concordance to his works it is a task of extreme difficulty at times to ascertain precisely what shade of meaning to assign to a word. The importance of Tertullian is becoming so widely recognised now that the task of compiling such a lexicon may be commended to a patient scholar as one of the most urgent requirements of Latin scholarship. But we shall never know his vocabulary and idiom in the way that it is possible to know that of Jerome, Augustine or Gregory. The comparative neglect of his works in the Middle Ages has resulted in the survival of a pathetically scanty list of good manuscripts. Much of his text will, in consequence, never be restored with absolute certainty.

The list of his surviving works, with the dates now generally [1] assigned to them, is as follows :—

Ad Martyras	Feb. or March 197.
Ad Nationes	after Feb. 197.
Apologeticus . . .	autumn 197.
De Testimonio Animae .	between 197 and 200.
De Spectaculis . . .	about 200
De Praescriptione Haereticorum .	about 200.
De Oratione	
De Baptismo	
De Patientia . . .	
De Paenitentia . . .	
De Cultu Feminarum .	between 200 and 206.
Ad Uxorem . . .	
Adversus Hermogenen .	
Adversus Iudaeos . .	
De Virginibus Velandis .	about 206.
Adversus Marcionem, Libri I.–IIII.	207–8.
De Pallio	209.

[1] I follow D'Alès, pp. xiii. ff., slightly different from Harnack, *Gesch. altchr. Litt.*, II. 2. (Leipzig, 1904), pp. 295 f.

Adversus Valentinianos   .   . ⎫
De Anima   .   .   .   . ⎪
De Carne Christi   .   .   . ⎪
De Resurrectione Carnis   .   . ⎬ between 208 and 211.
Adversus Marcionem, Liber V.   . ⎪
De Exhortatione Castitatis   . ⎭
De Corona   .   .   .   . 211.
Scorpiace .   .   .   .   . 211 or 212.
De Idololatria .   .   .   . 211 or 212.
Ad Scapulam .   .   .   . end of 212.

The following are definitely Montanist :—

De Fuga in Persecutione   .   . 213.
Adversus Praxean   .   .   . ⎫
De Monogamia .   .   .   . ⎬ after 213.
De Ieiunio   .   .   .   . ⎭
De Pudicitia   .   .   .   . between 217 and 222.

Besides these, several works by him have been lost. It is also to be noted that he issued the *Apologeticus* (probably) and the *De Spectaculis* (certainly) in Greek, as well as a Greek work on Baptism.

Of annotated editions of Tertullian's complete works, the best is that by Franciscus Oehler (Lipsiae, 3 Vols., 1853, 1854). The best text of the following works is to be found in the Vienna *Corpus Scriptorum Ecclesiasticorum Latinorum*, Vols. XX. and XLVII. (Vindobonae et Lipsiae, 1890, 1906) : *De Spectaculis, De Idololatria, Ad Nationes, De Testimonio Animae, Scorpiace, De Oratione, De Baptismo, De Pudicitia, De Ieiunio, De Anima, De Patientia, De Carnis Resurrectione, Adversus Hermogenen, Adversus Valentinianos, Adversus Omnes*

Haereses,[1] *Adversus Praxean*, *Adversus Marcionem*. The best work on the language of Tertullian is H. Hoppe, *Syntax und Stil des Tertullian* (Leipzig, 1903) ; on his theology, A. d'Alès, *La Théologie de Tertullien* (Paris, 1905) ; on his New Testament citations, H. Rönsch, *Das Neue Testament Tertullian's*, Leipzig, 1871.

I know no separate edition of the *De Oratione* ; the *De Baptismo* has been edited by J. M. Lupton (Cambridge, 1908).

De Oratione [2]

The *De Oratione* is of interest not only as the earliest surviving exposition of the Lord's Prayer in any language, but also for its intrinsic qualities, and the text of the prayer which it furnishes. The work does not seem to have been written for a polemical purpose, but merely for edification. Tertullian does not say from what Gospel he takes the Prayer, or indeed whether he takes it from the Gospels at all, but an examination of the text shows clearly that he follows the Matthaean, not the Lukan form. It is natural to compare the text as it appears here, with that furnished by Origen in his work, *On Prayer*. There is no marked difference, save that the petition "Thy Kingdom come" in Tertullian follows, and does not precede, "Thy will be done in heaven and in earth."

[1] This book is perhaps the work of Victorinus of Pettau († 303).

[2] The following works are of importance in this connexion: F. H. Chase, *The Lord's Prayer in the Early Church* [Texts and Studies, I. (3)], (Cambridge, 1891) ; von der Goltz, *Das Gebet in der ältesten Christenheit* (Leipzig, 1901); Dibelius, *Das Vaterunser* (Giessen, 1903) ; G. Walther, *Untersuchungen zur geschichte der griechischen Vaterunser-exegese* [Texte u. Untersuchungen, Bd. XL. (3)], Leipzig, 1914 ; W. Haller in *Zeitschr. f. prakt. Theologie*, Bd. XII. (1890), pp. 327–354. The last is exclusively concerned with our treatise.

The *De Oratione* is preserved as far as the beginning of Chap. XXI. in the Agobardine manuscript, Paris, Bibliothèque Nationale, MS. Latin 1622, of the ninth century, so called because it was once in the possession of the well-known Agobard, Bishop of Lyons (*ob.* 840). Chapters IX. to the end are preserved in a MS., formerly of the Irish foundation of Bobbio (near the Ticino) in northern Italy, now at the Ambrosian Library in Milan, G. 58 Sup., of the end of the tenth or the beginning of the eleventh century. No surviving manuscript presents it complete, but the edition of Martin Mesnart or of Jean Gagney, Lord High Almoner to François I. of France, which appeared in 1545 at Paris, must have been based on a manuscript of French *provenance*, in which it was unmutilated. Another lost manuscript contained the *De Oratione*, namely a *codex* belonging to Malmesbury,[1] which the English antiquary, John Leland, lent to Sigismund Gelenius for use in his Basle edition of Tertullian (1550).

De Baptismo

The *De Baptismo* is not merely the earliest treatise on its subject, but is the only Ante-Nicene treatise on any of the Sacraments, and though its occasion was controversial, it furnishes such exact information as we do not often have the good fortune to possess on such a subject. It is at the same time a treatise on Confirmation, because in those days Baptism and Confirmation "were regarded as two moments in a single action."[2]

---

[1] So I should, following Dr. M. R. James, interpret the *Masburensi*: see J. M. Lupton's edition of the *De Baptismo*, p. xxxvi.

[2] *Essays on the Early History of the Church and the Ministry*: by various writers, edited by H. B. Swete [and C. H. Turner] (London, 1918), p. 377 *n.* 2.

A Gnostic prophetess had denied the necessity for Baptism. She belonged to a branch of the Gnostics the name of which is doubtful. The manuscript tradition in Tertullian (Chap. I.) points to the expression "Gaiana heresis," which means a heresy founded by one Gaius; but the Jerome tradition, which undoubtedly refers to the same heresy, points to the title "Caina heresis."[1] The matter is of no great interest to us, except as giving Tertullian an opportunity to compose a treatise for the use of candidates for Baptism. It seems possible from the abruptness of the present beginning that the real beginning has been lost. The first part is a panegyric on water, in which much is worthily said on the simplicity of God's instruments, and there are collected many ingenious references to the importance of the element. The use of water in other religions and the valuable analogy thereby furnished to the cleansing of the soul are mentioned. He also brings unction and the laying on of hands under review. The central part of the treatise is devoted to the baptism of John, the question whether Jesus Himself baptized, and the further question, whether the apostles were baptized. The validity of heretical baptism is denied, and this part closes with a profoundly interesting section dealing with blood baptism or martyrdom. The concluding part discusses the ministry of Baptism, and defines what appears to be the attitude of the Universal Church at the time. The Bishop is the regular minister of Baptism. Presbyters and deacons also possess the right to baptize, as authorised by the Bishop. But the right belongs also to laymen, because what all have received, all may equally

---

[1] *Epist.* 69, § 1 (ed. Hilberg [C. S. E. L. LIV (1910)], p. 679, l. 6); *adv. Vigilant.*, § 8.

give.   Yet for the sake of peace, laymen are not to exercise their right except in cases of necessity and when there is a danger of the person's death.   Baptism by women is vehemently rejected.   Confirmation is the exclusive prerogative of the bishop.

B

TERTULLIAN'S TREATISES

CONCERNING PRAYER

JESUS CHRIST our Lord, God's Spirit,[1] God's Word and God's Reason,[2] Word of Reason and Reason of Word and Spirit of both, fixed for the new disciples of the new covenant a new form of prayer. For it was meet that in this sphere also new wine should be stored in new wine skins, and that a new patch should be sewn on a new garment. For everything that had been in the past, was either changed, as for example, Circumcision, or completed, as the rest of the Law, or fulfilled, like prophecy, or brought to perfection, as faith itself. All things were renewed from their carnal state and became spiritual by the new grace of God, which added the gospel to fulfil all that had been in the past. In it our Lord Jesus Christ was proved to be at once the Spirit of God, the Word of God and the Reason of God : the Spirit, by the power He had ; the Word, by His teaching ; and the Reason, by His coming. So, therefore, prayer as established by Christ consisted of

cf. John i. 1
cf. Rom. i. 4, etc.
cf. Matt. vi. 6 ff. ; Luke xi. 2
cf. Matt. ix. 17
cf. Matt. ix. 16
cf. Rom. ii. 29, etc.
cf. Matt. v. 17
cf. Matt. ii. 17, etc.
cf. Matt. v. 17
cf. John i. 1

---

[1] Elsewhere, also, Tertullian speaks of Christ as God's Spirit ; yet he distinguished the Three Persons of the Trinity.

[2] Tertullian was too good a Greek scholar not to know that the Greek word "Logos" (John i. 1) could not adequately be translated by one word in Latin. He therefore gives two renderings, "sermo" and "ratio," and, as if this were not enough, juggles with the two terms after he has given them. The later (European) rendering for "Logos" was "Verbum," not "Sermo."

three elements : the word, by which it is uttered ; the spirit, in which alone lies its power ; and the reason, by which it is taught. "John," too, "had taught" his disciples to pray, but all John's work was a preparation for Christ, until when He (Christ) had increased—even as the same John prophesied that He must increase, while he himself must decrease—all the work of the earlier servant must pass along with his spirit itself to his Master. The reason, too, why there is no surviving record of the words in which John taught his followers to pray, is this, that the earthly yielded to the heavenly. "He that is of the earth," He said, "speaketh earthly things, and He that is here from heaven, speaketh those things that He hath seen." And what is there belonging to the Lord Christ that is not from heaven—this training in prayer included? Let us consider therefore, blessed ones, His heavenly wisdom, particularly that touching the precept to pray in secret, in which He both exacted man's faith, his trust that both the sight and the hearing of the all-powerful God are present within the house and even in a secret place, and also longed for the obedience of faith, so that man should offer his worship to Him alone, who he was confident sees and hears everywhere. The second wisdom set forth in the second precept would have a like connexion with faith and the obedience of faith, if we did not think a volume of words necessary for our approach to the Lord, who we are certain looks to the good of His own without any action of ours. And yet this brevity, because it conduces to the attainment of the third degree of wisdom, is sup-ported by the substance of a great and blessed interpre-tation, and is as comprehensive in thought as it is succinct in language. For it includes not only the special duties of prayer, namely the worship of God or the petition of man, but almost the whole of the Lord's teaching, all the recollection of His training, so that really in the prayer there is contained an epitome of the whole Gospel.

2. It begins with witness to God and the reward of faith, when we say: FATHER, WHO ART IN HEAVEN. For we are both praying to God and setting forth our faith, the reward of which is the right to call Him by this name. It is written: "To them that have believed in Him, He hath given the power to be called sons of God." And yet the Lord frequently declared God to be our Father, and even commanded that we were to call none Father on earth save Him whom we have in heaven. Therefore in worshipping Him thus we are also obeying a command. Happy they who recognise their Father! It is the failure to do this that is cast in the teeth of Israel, a failure to which the Spirit calls heaven and earth to witness, saying, "I have begotten sons, and they have not recognised me." And in calling Him Father, we name Him God also. This name indicates at once His regard for us and His power. Also, in calling on the Father, we are calling upon the Son, for He says: "I and the Father are one." Nor is the Mother,[1] the Church, overlooked either, since in "son" and "father" "mother" is implied, from whom the names both of father and of son derive their meaning. In one way, therefore, or in one word we at once honour God in company with His own[2] and remember the command, and stigmatise those that have forgotten the Father.

3. The name of God the Father had been revealed to no one. Even he who had asked about it—I mean

Matt. vi.9

John i. 12

cf. Matt. vi. 1, etc.
cf. Matt. xxiii. 9

Isa. i. 2

John x. 30
cf. Gal. iv. 26

---

[1] This is possibly the earliest reference to the Church as Mother (cf. Gal. iv. 26), and it is characteristically fantastic.
[2] That is, the Son and the Church.

cf. Exod.
iii. 13, 14
cf. Matt.
xi. 27
John v.
43
John xii.
28
John
xvii. 6
cf. Matt.
vi. 9
Moses—had really been told a different name. It has been revealed to us in the Son. But who, then, is the Son? It is a new name of the Father. "I have come," said He, "in the name of the Father"; and again, "Father, glorify Thy name"; and more clearly, "I manifested Thy name unto men." We ask, therefore, that it should be kept holy, not because it is becoming that men should pray for God's good, as if there were also another power for whose good we could pray Him, or as if He would be in trouble if we did not pray for Him. It is, of course, most fitting that God should be blessed everywhere and always for the remembrance of His benefits—a remembrance due at all times from every man. This, too, takes the place of blessing. But when is God's name not holy and hallowed in itself, seeing that its power makes all others holy? Before His presence the surrounding angels never cease to say: Rev. iv.
8 "Holy, holy, holy." So, therefore, we too, candidates for the position of angel, if we earn it, even in this world can fully learn that heavenly word with which to address God, and the duty pertaining to our future state of glory. So far concerning God's glory. Again, as regards our Matt. vi.
9 petition, when we say: HALLOWED BE THY NAME, we ask that it should be made holy in us, who are in Him, and at the same time in all others, on whom the grace of God is still waiting, that we may obey this precept cf. Matt.
v. 44 also, by praying for all, even for our enemies. And therefore, by curtailing our utterance and by refraining from cf. Matt.
vi. 9 saying "let it be hallowed *in us*," we mean "*in all*."

Matt. vi.
10 4. In accordance with this form we add: THY WILL BE DONE IN HEAVEN AND IN EARTH, not because any one is opposing the doing of God's will, and we are praying that He may see His will triumph, but we ask

that His will may be done in all. For by a figurative interpretation as flesh and spirit, we are "earth" and "heaven." And yet even if the petition is to be understood in its plain sense, nevertheless it has the same meaning, that in us God's will may be done on earth, and that, of course, it may be done in heaven also. What else does God will but that we should walk according to His training? We ask, therefore, that He supply us with the nature and power of His will, that we may be safe both in heaven and on earth, because the chief purpose of His will is the salvation of those whom He has adopted. There is also that will of God which the Lord carried out in preaching, working and enduring. For if He Himself declared that He was cf. John doing not His own will, but His Father's, without doubt vi. 38, 39 His deeds were in accordance with His Father's will. These we are now incited to regard as patterns, that we may both preach and work and endure even to death. Such an ideal we cannot attain independently of the will of God. Likewise when we say, "Thy will be Matt. vi. done," even in that petition we are praying for our own 10 benefit, because there is no evil in God's will, in spite of the fact that each man is rewarded according to his merits. By the use of this phrase we give ourselves a timely warning that may help us to endure. Even the Lord, when in view of His impending passion He was fain to show the weakness of the flesh even in His own flesh, said: "Father, let this cup pass from me," and then remembering, added: "but let not My Luke will, but Thine be done." He Himself was the will and xxii. 42 power of the Father, and yet to show the endurance that became Him, He delivered Himself to the Father's will.

5. THY KINGDOM COME is also closely bound up with the petition: "Thy will be done." It means *in us*, of course. For when does God not reign, "in whose hand is the heart of all kings"? But whatever we pray for for ourselves, we assign to Him, and we attribute to Him what we expect from Him. Therefore if the reality of the Lord's Kingdom is bound up with God's will and our expectation, how is it that certain persons seek it in some period of the present world's history, whereas the Kingdom of God, for the coming of which we pray, looks to the end of the world? We are eager to enter into our Kingdom: we do not want to serve too long. Even if the request for the coming of the Kingdom had not been prescribed in the prayer, we would of our own accord have proffered that petition in our haste to embrace our hope. The souls of the martyrs under the altar call aloud to the Lord in their displeasure: "How long wilt Thou not avenge our blood, O Lord, on the inhabitants of the earth?" Of course their avenging is settled to take place at the end of the world. Nay, rather, the speedy coming of Thy Kingdom, O Lord, means to the Christians answered prayer, to the heathen disgrace, to the angels rapture: for its sake we are tormented; nay, rather, for its sake we pray.

6. But how finely the Divine wisdom has arranged the order of the prayer, in making room, after heavenly things—that is, after the name of God, the will of God and the Kingdom of God—for a petition for earthly needs also! For the Lord had also given the command: "Seek first the Kingdom, and then these things also will be added unto you." And yet we ought rather to understand GIVE US OUR DAILY BREAD THIS DAY in a spiritual sense. For "our bread" is Christ, because

Christ is life and the bread of life : "I am," He says, John vi.
"the bread of life," and a little earlier : " bread is the $\frac{35}{}$ John vi.
word of the living God, that descendeth from heaven " ; 33
and further, because His body is also deemed to be in
the bread : [1] "This is My body." Therefore in asking Matt.
daily bread we ask to live perpetually in Christ and xxvi. 26 Luke
undivided from His body. But because this phrase is xxii. 19
admitted in a carnal sense, it cannot be realised without 1 Cor. xi. 24
the piety that belongs to spiritual instruction as well.
For He commands that bread be sought, which is all the
faithful need ; " for after all other things do the heathen Matt. vi.
seek." It is this He insists on by examples and also 32
discusses in parables, when He says : "Does a father Matt. xv.
take away the bread from his children and hand it over 26
to dogs?" Also : "Does he give a stone to his son Matt. vii.
when he asks for bread ?" He shows, you see, what sons 9
expect from a father. But the man who knocked at the cf. Luke
door "in the night" also called for bread. Christ, xi. 5
further, was quite right to add : "Give us this day," Matt. vi.
seeing He had said beforehand : [2] "Ponder not about the 11 Matt. vi.
morrow, what ye shall eat." In conformity with this 34
teaching He added the parable of the man who planned cf. Luke
an enlargement of his "granaries" for his increasing xii. 16–20
crops, and periods of long freedom from care, but died
on that very "night."

7. It followed that, having noted the generosity of
God, we should beg for His mercy also. For what good

---

[1] J. J. Blunt, *The Right Use of the Early Fathers* (London, 1857),
p. 568, renders : "in the bread is understood his Body" ; D'Alès,
Théologie de Tertullien," p. 366, takes the meaning to be : "the
Body of Christ also is classed within the category of bread, is one
kind (among others) of bread."

[2] That is, earlier in the Sermon on the Mount. Tertullian's
memory is at fault, for the passage actually occurs later than the
Lord's Prayer, namely, at Matt. vi. 34.

will nourishment do, if we are allotted to Him exactly as a bull is to sacrifice?[1] The Lord knew that He alone was "without sin." He teaches us, therefore, to ask that "*our* debts be forgiven us." Confession is the asking of indulgence, because he who asks indulgence, is confessing sin. So, also, penitence is shown to be acceptable to God, because "He wishes it more than the death of the sinner." "Debt," moreover, is in the Scriptures a figure for sin, because, like debt, sin is due to be judged and a demand is made on it, and it does not escape just exaction, unless exaction be remitted; even as the master "forgave" that slave "the debt." For that is the lesson running through the whole parable. The fact, too, that the same slave, though freed by his master, does not in like manner spare his own debtor, and for that reason is brought before his master, and "handed over to the torturer" "to pay the last penny"— by which is meant punishment for even a slight sin— that fact is connected with our promise also to forgive our debtors. Already in another place, in accordance with this style of prayer, he says: "Forgive, and it shall be forgiven you"; and when Peter asked "whether a brother was to be forgiven seven times," He said: "Nay, rather seventy times seven," that He might remodel and improve the law by which in Genesis "vengeance over Cain" was reckoned "seven times, but over Lamech seventy times seven."[2]

8. To the fullness of so comprehensive a prayer He made the addition, that we might make entreaty not only for the forgiveness of sins, but also for their entire

---

[1] That is, if we are handed over to nourishment to be fattened thereby.

[2] There seems no doubt that the passage of Genesis was in Our Lord's mind, as Tertullian states.

removal: LEAD US NOT INTO TEMPTATION; in other words, "Do not allow us to be deceived, of course by 'him who tempts.'" But away with the idea that the Lord should be thought to tempt, as if He either did not know each man's faith or was eager to dethrone it. Weakness and evil nature belong to the devil. For even the command to Abraham about the sacrificing of his son was made not to try his faith, but to approve it, that in Abraham the Lord might furnish an example for the carrying out of the command, which He was afterwards to issue, that none should look upon his dear ones with greater love than upon his God. He Himself, when tempted by the devil, pointed out the ruler and author of temptation. This clause He enforces by later words, saying: "Pray that ye be not tempted." They were so tempted in abandoning their Lord, because they had given themselves up to sleep rather than to prayer. Therefore the clause brings the answer, explaining what is meant by: "Lead us not into temptation." For this is what it means: BUT DRAW US AWAY FROM THE EVIL ONE.

[margin references: Matt. vi. 13 cf. I Thess. iii. 5 cf. Jas. i. 13 cf. Gen. xxii. 2 cf. Matt. x. 37 cf. Matt. iv. 10 Luke xxii. 46 cf. Luke xxii. 45 Matt. vi. 13 Matt. vi. 13]

9. How many commands of prophets, gospels, apostles, how many words of the Lord, parables, illustrations, precepts are alluded to in abbreviated form in very few words! How many duties are fully set forth all at once! Respect to God in the Father, witness to faith in His name, offering of obedience in the will, mention of hope in the Kingdom, desire for life in bread, confession of debts in prayer for forgiveness, anxiety about temptations in the request for protection! What wonder? God alone could teach how He wished prayer to be addressed to Him. The ritual of prayer, therefore, having been settled by Himself and inspired by its own special law from His own spirit even at the very time when it was

coming forth from the divine lips, ascends to Heaven, recommending to the Father what the Son taught.

10. Since, however, the Lord who has regard to human needs, says separately, after communicating the set form of prayer : "Ask, and ye shall receive," and since there are things to be asked in view of the circumstances of each individual, they that approach have the right, after dispatching first the regular and standard prayer by way of a foundation, to build on it outside petitions embodying their desires, always remembering, however, the prescribed requests.

11. Lest we should be as far away from the ears of God as we are from His precepts, the recollection of the precepts paves the way to heaven for our prayers ; the chief of these precepts is that we should not ascend to God's altar until we make an end of any disagreement or misdemeanour of which we have been guilty towards our brethren. For what sort of behaviour is it to approach the peace of God without peace in one's heart ! to ask the forgiveness of debts while we withhold forgiveness ourselves ! how will he who is angry with his brother appease his Father, seeing that all wrath has from the beginning been forbidden us? Even Joseph, when giving his brothers permission to go and fetch their father, said : "And do not fall into anger by the way." He certainly warned us at that time—for elsewhere our rule of life is named "The Way"—not to proceed to the Father in company with anger, when we are on the way of prayer. Then the Lord, manifestly enlarging the law, puts wrath against one's brother into the same category as murder. He does not permit injury to be requited even in word :[1] even if we must

---

[1] Reading *malum* for *malo*.

get into a passion, our anger is not to be maintained
beyond sunset, as the Apostle warns us. And how cf. Eph.
reckless it is either to pass a day without prayer, iv. 26
while you are slow to apologise to your brother, or
to lose the chance to pray while your angry temper
persists !

12. And it is not from anger only, but from every
possible clouding of the spirit that the purpose of prayer
ought to be free, since that purpose proceeds from a
spirit like unto that Spirit to which it is directed. For
a spirit that is stained cannot possibly be recognised by
a holy spirit, or a sad by a joyful or a shackled by a free
spirit. No one welcomes an adversary, and only a real
friend is admitted to our confidence.

13. But what sense is there in engaging in prayer,
with hands washed, it is true, but with spirit befouled,
since even for the hands themselves spiritual cleanliness
is necessary, that they may be raised in a state of purity
from forgery, from murder, from cruelty, from poisonings,
from idolatry and all other stains, which are devised by
the spirit, though they are carried out by the work of the
hands? This is the true cleanliness, and not that which
very many superstitiously cultivate, making use of water
for every prayer, even when they have just bathed the
whole body. When I inquired very carefully about it
and asked the reason, I found that it was a commemora-
tion of the fact that Pilate washed his hands when cf. Matt.
delivering up the Lord. But we worship the Lord, we xxvii. 24
are not delivering Him up; nay, rather, we ought to
oppose the example of such an one, and not for that
reason to wash our hands. Except we wash (for conscience sake) on account of some stain due to a human
manner of life, in other respects our hands are clean

enough, for we have washed them (with the rest of our bodies), once for all in Christ.

14. Although Israel wash daily over his whole body, yet he is never clean. At least, his hands are always unclean, for they are covered over for ever with the blood of the prophets and of the Lord Himself; and therefore, inheriting the guilt of their fathers, they do not dare even to raise them to the Lord, lest some Isaiah should cry aloud, lest Christ should be filled with horror. We, however, do not merely raise them, but also spread them out, and we make our confession to Christ, while we represent the Lord's passion and likewise pray.

15. But since we have touched upon one kind of useless worship, it will not be irksome to point out others also, which are justly to be reproached as useless, since they are practised without the authority of any command either of the Lord or of the apostles. Such practices are, indeed, to be put down not to piety, but to superstition, being as they are eagerly pursued and forced, the product of a scrupulous rather than a rational sense of duty, and assuredly to be stopped if for no other reason than that they put us on a level with the heathen. For example, certain people offer prayer divested of their upper garments ; that is the way the heathen approach their images. If this were our duty, the apostles who give instruction regarding the attitude of prayer, would certainly have included it in their teaching ; but perhaps some suppose that Paul "left his upper garment with Carpus" while engaged in prayer ! God, of course, would not listen to men clad in the upper garments although He caught the words of the three holy men

cf. 2 Tim. iv. 13

cf. Dan. iii. 88, 21

in the Babylonian king's furnace, when they prayed with their trousers and their turbans on ! [1]

16. Again, why, after prayer is duly ended, certain people are accustomed to seat themselves, I cannot see the reason, unless it is that which appeals to children. For, if the well-known Hermas, whose writing is generally entitled " The Shepherd," [2] had not " seated himself on his couch " after his prayer was over, cf. Herm. vis. v. 1. but had done something else, would we claim that this practice, too, should be observed ? Certainly not. For even now the words : " When I had prayed and had seated myself upon my couch," are set down Herm. vis. v. 1 simply in the course of the narrative, and not as a pattern of a custom to be followed. Otherwise, prayer will have to be offered only where there is a couch. Nay, any one who sits on a seat or a bench will be acting contrary to Scripture. But, since the heathen do likewise, sitting down after they have prayed to their marionettes, [3] even for that reason what is performed in the presence of images deserves to be reproved in us. Thereto is added the fault of irreverence, a fault that even the heathen themselves would

---

[1] Tertullian in such treatises as these generally restrains the tendency to humour, which finds such vent in the *Apology*.

[2] Hermas was brother of Pius, bishop of Rome from about A.D. 140–155. He wrote a lengthy apocalyptic work in Greek called *The Shepherd*. It is somewhat strange that in certain churches this work should have acquired something like ''canonical'' authority about the end of the second century. Two early translations into Latin were made, both of which, as well as the original Greek, are still extant : editions of the Greek, for example, by O. v. Gebhardt and A. v. Harnack (Lipsiæ, 1877) and A. Lelong (Paris, 1912), the latter with French translation, etc. Already in the third century the book was deprived of all canonicity : see the writer's *Text and Canon of the New Testament* (London, 1913), p. 180.

[3] This term *sigillaria* is purposely used by Tertullian to show his contempt for the images of the pagan gods.

understand, if they had any sense. If indeed it is irreverent to be seated in close view of, and right opposite him whom you are at the very moment revering and worshipping, how much more is this act irreligious in close view of the living God, while the messenger of prayer[1] is still standing by! Unless it be that we are reproaching God with the weariness prayer causes us.

17. And yet if we pray in an orderly and humble attitude, we shall the more commend our prayers to God, even if our hands themselves are not raised on high, but raised moderately and fitly, without the presumptuous raising of the face either. For the publican in the Gospel, who not only prayed with humble words but with humble and downcast expression of face, "went away more justified than" the self-confident Pharisee. Even the tones of the voice ought to be subdued; else how many air passages should we need, if we be heard for our sound! But God is hearer not of the voice, but of the mind,[2] even as He is its discerner. The demon of the Pythian oracle says: "Even a dumb man I understand, and I catch the utterance of one that does not speak."[3] Is it a sound that God's ears are waiting for? How then could

cf. 1 Tim. ii. 8

cf. Luke xviii. 14

cf. Herod. i. 47

---

[1] The belief that human prayers were conveyed by angels or messengers from man to God was inherited by Christians from Judaism.

[2] This remarkable expression is repeated by Cyprian, *De Dominica Oratione*, c. 4 (ed. Hartel, p. 209, l. 6), and by Ambrosiaster (Pseudo-Augustine), *Quæstiones Veteris et Novi Testamenti CXXVII*. 18, § 1 (ed. Souter, p. 45, l. 8).

[3] Crœsus, King of Lydia, consulted various oracles concerning the growing power of the Persians. Herodotus (I. 47) gives five hexameters as constituting the reply of the Pythian priestess of Apollo at Delphi. It is the second line that Tertullian refers to; to the third and fourth he refers in his *Apologeticus*, c. 22.

Jonah's prayer find its way out to heaven from the depths of the sea monster's belly through the inward parts of so great a beast, and from the very depths of the sea through so great a mass of waters? What more will those who pray too loudly gain, except the disturbance of their neighbours? Nay rather, if they reveal their petitions, what less are they doing than if they were to pray in public?

cf. Jon. ii. 11

18. Another custom has now become increasingly common. Those who are fasting, after engaging in prayer with their brethren, refrain from offering the kiss of peace, which is the seal of prayer. But when can peace be more fittingly exchanged with the brethren than at the time when the prayer of fasting is ascending and is more acceptable, that they themselves may share in our fasting, by which they have been softened for the making of an agreement with a brother touching their own peace?[1] What prayer is complete when divorced from the holy kiss? Who when performing his duty to the Lord, is hindered by peace? What sort of a sacrifice is it from which one departs without peace! Whatever[2] sort of prayer it be, it will not be better than obedience to the precept which commands us to conceal our fastings. As it is, by abstaining from the kiss, we are recognised to be fasting. But if there is anything to be said for the practice, you can, perhaps, to prevent you from being guilty of disobeying this command, dispense with the kiss of peace at home,

cf. Matt. vi. 16 f.

---

[1] Tertullian means that at the time of our fasting the kiss of peace communicates blessing to our brethren, and that this influence disposes them the better to be at peace with us. It is, however, by no means certain at this point what the true text is.

[2] This sentence contains an objection put into the mouth of the person who seeks to dispense with the kiss. What follows contains Tertullian's rejoinder to this objection.

C

where fasting cannot be entirely concealed. Wherever else, however, you can conceal your state of fasting, you ought to remember the precept; you will thus carry out the public practice and the private custom alike. So also on Good Friday, on which the religious duty of fasting is general, and as it were official, we rightly give up the kiss, not being careful to conceal what we are doing in common with everybody else.

19. Similarly, also, with regard to the days of the stations,[1] very many do not think that they should take part in the prayers of the sacrifices,[2] because the station ought to be broken up after receiving the Lord's body.[3] Does the Eucharist, then, abolish a service dedicated to God, or does it not rather bind it the more to God? Will not your station be more instinct with religion, if you also stand at God's altar?[4] If you have received and preserved[5] the Lord's body, both privileges are secure, your participation in the sacrifice and your performance of your duty. If the station has got its name from the example of the army (for we are also the soldiers of God), assuredly no joy or sorrow happening to the camp abolishes the

[1] I have kept the word "stations" as representing the Latin *stationes*, in spite of its unfamiliarity in this sense. The use is a metaphor from the military sense, as Tertullian himself recognises. Christ's soldiers are as it were on outpost duty. *Stationes* were fixed fasts, or half-fasts, observed on two days of the week, *feria quarta* (Wednesday) and *feria sexta* (Friday). The fast was broken at the ninth hour of the day, corresponding to 3 p.m. at the equinoxes. The earliest mention of the *statio* is in The Shepherd of Hermas (*Simil.* V. 1, §§ 1, 2, where the language shows that the term was then new in that sense).

[2] He is here alluding to fastings and the Eucharist. The prayers themselves are sacrifices (cf. *Apol.* 30, with Mayor's note, and *Orat.* 27, 28, below.)

[3] Each *statio* concluded with the Eucharist.

[4] That is, "the communion table," on which the elements were placed : at this period there were no stone altars in the churches.

[5] An early reference to Reservation of the Sacrament.

outpost duty of the soldiers ; for joy will carry out the discipline more gladly, and sorrow more anxiously.

20. Again, concerning the dress, of women at least, the variety of custom has made it impertinent, especially for a man of no position like myself, to express misgivings, after what the holy Apostle has said, except that there would be nothing impertinent in the statement of scruples if they were in accordance with the Apostle's views. Concerning the propriety, indeed, of dress and adornment there is an unmistakable direction from Peter also, checking in the same words because also in the same spirit, as Paul, both the flaunting of dress, the arrogant display of gold, and the meretriciously elaborate coiffure.

cf. 1 Cor. xi. 5 ; cf. 1 Tim. ii. 9

cf. 1 Pet. iii. 3

21. A practice, however, maintained universally throughout the churches, must be reviewed as if it were of doubtful validity, namely, whether virgins ought to be veiled [1] or not. Those who concede to virgins the right to keep their heads unveiled, appear to rely on the fact that the Apostle laid it down not that virgins specifically, but that women should be veiled, and referred not to the sex, employing the word " females," but to the rank of the sex, saying " women."   For if he had named the sex, using the word " females," he would clearly have laid down the law with regard to every woman ; but when he names one rank of the sex, he distinguishes the other from it by his silence. " He could," they say, " have either named virgins specially, or used the comprehensive general term, 'females.'"

cf. 1 Cor. xi. 6, etc.

22. Those who make this concession should reflect on the constitution of the word itself.   What is meant by the term " woman " from the very earliest literature in the holy writings?   They find that already it is the name

---

[1] Tertullian afterwards wrote a special treatise on this subject, *De Virginibus Velandis.*

of the sex, and does not indicate the rank in the sex;
since Eve, when she had not yet known man, was named
by God both "woman" and "female," "female" in virtue
of her sex in a general sense, "woman" in virtue of the
rank of her sex in a special sense. So, since Eve was
called by the name "woman," though at that time still
unmarried, that name has become applicable to a virgin
also. And it is not to be wondered at that the Apostle,
being of course moved by the same spirit as inspired the
composition of the whole of the divine Scripture, includ-
ing the book of Genesis also, used the same word
"woman" as, after the example of Eve, is suitable to an
unmarried woman and a virgin. Besides, the rest of his
doctrine is in agreement. For by the very fact that he
did not name virgins, any more than in another passage,
where he is teaching about marriage, he sufficiently declares that he has been speaking about every woman and
about the whole sex, and that he has made no distinction
between woman and virgin; the latter, as a matter of fact,
he does not name. One who remembers to make a distinction in other passages, where of course a difference
demands it,—and he shows the distinction by indicating
each of the two classes by its own name,—when he does
not make a distinction, while he refrains from naming
both, intends that no difference should be understood.
Again, in the Greek language, in which the Apostle composed his letters, it is the custom to speak as much of
"women" as of "females." If, therefore, this word,
which is in the translation instead of "female," is in frequent use as the name of the sex, it was the sex he named,
when he said "woman." In the sex, moreover, the virgin
is also referred to. But the following statement is also
clear: "Every woman," he says, "that prays or preaches

cf. Gen.
ii. 22, 23

cf. 1 Cor.
xi. 5

cf. 1 Cor.
vii. 1, 4

cf. 1 Cor.
vii. 25,
etc.

1 Cor. xi.
5

with uncovered head, disgraces her head." What is
meant by "every woman," if not women of every age,
every class, every position? By the use of the word "all,"
he leaves out no element in woman, just as he leaves out
no element in man, and no aspect of veiling; for he says
in like manner: "every man." Therefore, just as in the   1 Cor. xi.
case of the male sex, under the name "man" even a   4
beardless man is forbidden to veil himself, so also in the
case of the female sex, under the name "woman" even
the virgin is commanded to be veiled. In both sexes
alike let the younger follow the practice of the elder, or
else let the male virgins be veiled too, if the female virgins are not veiled, because the male virgins are not bound
by name either; let a man who is also beardless, be
regarded as different (from another), if a woman who is
also a virgin, is to be so regarded. To be sure it is "on   1 Cor. xi.
account of the angels," he says, that they ought to be   10
veiled, because the angels revolted from God for the sake Gen. vi. 2
of "the daughters of men." [1] Who, then, would claim
that women alone—that is, those already married, who
have done with virginity—are objects of desire, unless it
be unlawful that virgins also should excel in beauty and
find lovers? Nay, rather, let us see whether it was not
virgins only that they desired, since the Scripture says:
"The daughters of men," because the writer could have   Gen. vi. 2
named "wives of men" or "women" indifferently. Also
in saying: "And took them to themselves as wives," his   Gen. vi. 2

---

[1] Genesis vi. 2, according to the Greek (and Old Latin) Bible,
reads: "that *the angels* of God saw the daughters of men that they
were fair," etc. This mistranslation gave rise to a widespread belief
that there were angels who were themselves actuated by lust, and
could inspire it in women. The offspring of these early unions were
believed to be giants. It was also believed that the evil spirits or
demons were similarly descended (Justin, *Apol.* II. 5; Tert., *Apol.*
22, with Mayor's notes).

view is determined by the fact that it is those, of course, that are free,[1] who are taken as wives. He would have expressed himself differently concerning those that are not free. Of course they are apart alike from widowhood and virginity. So by naming the sex in general terms "daughters," he mingled the subdivisions together in the whole class. Also, when he says that "Nature herself teaches" that women ought to be veiled, by assigning the hair as a covering and an adornment to women, is not the same covering and the same glory of the head assigned also to virgins? "If it is a disgrace to a woman to be shaved," it is equally so to a virgin. From those, then, to whom one state of the head is assigned, one practice with regard to the head is also demanded, and this applies even to those virgins who are protected by their childhood; for from the very first she has been named "female." This, finally, is also the practice of Israel. But even if he did not practise it, our law, being enlarged and completed, would claim the addition for itself. He (or it) would be excused if he (or it) cast the veil over virgins also. Now let the age which knows not its own sex, retain the privilege belonging to its simplicity. For Eve and Adam also, when "knowledge" befell them, immediately "covered" what they had recognised. Certainly those in whom childhood has now passed away, ought in adolescence to perform the duties of morality as well as those of nature. For both in body and in duties they are counted among women. No woman is a virgin from the time that she is marriageable, since the age in her has already married its own husband, namely time. But some virgin has vowed herself to God. Yet from that time she both dresses her hair differently and

---

[1] *i.e.* unmarried, not yet married.

changes all her dress to that of a woman.   Let her then
make a complete profession and present all the charac-
teristics of a virgin ; let her completely enshroud that
which for God's sake she conceals.   It is of importance
to us to commend to the knowledge of God alone what
the grace of God makes it possible to practise, lest we
should esteem as highly what comes from men, as what
we hope for from God.   Why dost thou bare before God
what thou coverest before men ?   Wilt thou be more
modest in public than in church ?   If it is a gift of God,
and "thou hast received it, why dost thou boast," he 1 Cor. iv.
asks, "as if thou hadst not received it "?   Why by self- 7
display dost thou pass a judgment on other women ?   Is
thy ostentation meant to encourage others to that which
is good ?   But really if thou boastest, thou art thyself in
danger of loss, and thou art also forcing others into the
same dangers.   If we assume a quality from a passion
for glory, we are liable to be deceived.   Veil thyself,
virgin, if virgin thou art ; for modesty is thy duty.   If
thou art a virgin, do not submit to the gaze of the multitude.   Let no one look with admiration on thy form ; let
no one feel thy falsehood.[1]   Thou counterfeitest well the
aspect of a bride, if so be thou dost veil thy head.   Nay,
thou dost not appear false ; for thou hast wedded Christ.
To Him thou hast surrendered thy flesh ; act as thy Husband's rule requires.   If He bids brides of others to veil
themselves, be sure he bids His own much more.   But
think not that the rule of every predecessor is to be upset.
Many give over their own wisdom and its steadfastness
to the bondage of another's habit.   Let them not,
then, be forced to veil themselves, but at any rate it

---

[1] The " falsehood " of women means the appearance (without the
reality) of being a *married* woman.

is not right that those who wish to do so should be prevented. Even those who cannot deny that they are virgins I permit to enjoy in their repute[1] quietness of conscience before God. Concerning those, however, who are promised to bridegrooms, I can unhesitatingly go beyond my rule and declare with all solemnity that they must be veiled from that day on which they have quivered at their first contact with a man's body in kiss and right hand. For everything in them has already entered into wedlock, their age by its ripeness, their flesh by its age, their spirit by its knowledge, their modesty by its experience of the kiss, their hope by its expectation, their mind by its consent. Rebecca is enough of an example for us, who when her bridegroom had been merely pointed out, "veiled herself" when marrying the knowledge of him.[2]

cf. Gen. xxiv. 65

23. As regards kneeling also, prayer finds a variety of practice in the action of a certain very few who refrain from kneeling on the Saturday.[3] At the very moment when this difference of opinion is pleading its cause in the churches, the Lord will give His grace that they may either yield or, without proving a stumbling-block to others, follow their own opinion. But we, according to the tradition we have received, on the day of the Lord's resurrection, and on it alone, ought to refrain carefully not only from this, but from every attitude and duty that cause perplexity, putting off even our daily business, "lest we give any place to the devil." The same thing,

cf. Eph. iv. 27

---

[1] Text and interpretation alike are here uncertain.

[2] This very striking expression means that in having come to know him who was to be her husband, she has already as it were entered into wedlock.

[3] Latin *sabbato*. I have avoided "Sabbath" as a translation because of the frequent incorrect use of it nowadays for "Sunday."

too, at Whitsuntide, which is distinguished by the same solemnity of its rejoicing. But who would hesitate daily to prostrate himself before God even at the very first prayer with which we enter on the day? Further, at the fastings and stations no prayer must be engaged in without the bended knee and the other signs of humility. For we are not only praying, but also begging for mercy and confessing our misdeeds to God our Lord. With regard to the times of prayer nothing at all has been ordained, save of course that we must pray at all times and "in all places." [1 Tim. ii. 8]

24. But why "in all places," when we are forbidden to do so in public? "In all places," he means, that convenience or even necessity has offered. Nor indeed do we regard the apostles as having disobeyed this command, when they prayed and sang to God in prison in the hearing of the prisoners, or Paul, who on board ship "in the presence of all celebrated the Eucharist."[1] [1 Tim. ii. 8; 1 Tim. ii. 8; cf. Acts xvi. 25; Acts xxvii. 35]

25. Concerning time, however, the keeping also of certain hours will not be useless from an external point of view—I mean of these common hours that mark the intervals of the day, the third, sixth and ninth,[2] which in Scripture are to be found the most usual. The first pouring of the Holy Spirit on the assembled disciples took place at the third hour. Peter, on the day on which he experienced the vision of all uncleanness in the vessel, had "at the sixth hour ascended to the top of the house to pray." "He also in company with John was on his way into the temple at the ninth hour," when [cf. Acts ii. 15; cf. Acts x. 9; cf. Acts iii. 1]

---

[1] That Tertullian means this by *eucharistiam fecit* is confirmed by Cyprian, *Epist.* 70, § 2 (p. 768, l. 19, Hartel).

[2] According to the usual practice in the early centuries of the Church; the scriptural instances he proceeds to give.

he restored the paralytic [1] to health.   And although these facts are stated simply without any command about the practice, yet it would be a good thing to establish some prior standard which will both compel the remembrance of prayer, and as it were compulsorily at times drag one away from affairs to such a duty.   We read also of Daniel's practice, which followed, you may be sure, the teaching of Israel : we ought, like him, to pray not less than thrice a day, being debtors to the three, Father, Son, and Holy Spirit ; of course, quite apart from the regular prayers which without any reminder are due at the beginning of day and night.   But it becomes the faithful neither to take food nor to proceed to the bath before prayer has intervened : for the refreshment and food of the spirit must be deemed to come before that of the flesh, since heavenly things come before earthly things.

26. When a brother has entered thy house, suffer him not to depart without prayer ("Thou hast seen," says he, "a brother, thou hast seen thy Lord "),[2] particularly if he be a stranger, lest perchance he be an angel.   Even he himself, when received by brethren, would not put earthly refreshment before heavenly.   For immediately your faith will be judged.   Or else how will you say according to the precept: "Peace be to this house," if

cf. Dan. vi. 10

Apo-
cryph.
(Resch,
Agrapha[2],
p. 182,
No. 144
[L. 65])
cf. Heb.
xiii. 2
Luke x. 5

---

[1] Tertullian's memory has played him false here : the man was "lame" (Acts iii. 2), not a paralytic.

[2] The manner in which Tertullian quotes this sentence shows that for him it had the value of Holy Scripture.   Yet it is impossible for us even to state from what book it comes.   Clement of Alexandria twice (*Stromateis*, I. 19, § 94 ; II. 15, § 71) quotes it in Greek in almost the identical words.   It has been remarked that the juxtaposition of the two clauses, where the first has the value of a subordinate clause, points to a Hebrew or Aramaic original.   For the thought compare Matt. xxv. 40.

you do not exchange a greeting of peace with those also who are in the house?

27. Those who are more careful in the matter of prayer, are wont to add in their prayers the "Hallelu- Rev. xix. jah" and psalms of this character, to the clauses of 1, etc. which a response is to be made by those who are in their company. And certainly every custom is excellent which conduces to the precedence and honour of God, and such is the bringing to Him a full prayer like some fat victim.

28. This is in fact the spiritual victim that abolished the sacrifices of the olden time. "To what purpose," Isa. i. 11, says He, "is the multitude of your sacrifices unto Me? 12 I am full of the burnt offerings of rams, and I will have none of the fat of lambs or the blood of bulls and of goats. For who hath required these at your hands?" What God, therefore, did seek, the Gospel teaches. "The hour will come," He says, "when true worshippers John iv. shall worship the Father in spirit and truth." For "God 23, 24 is a Spirit," and therefore "He seeks worshippers of like kind." We are the true worshippers and the true priests, who praying with the spirit, with the spirit sacrifice prayer, a victim specially appropriate and acceptable to God, a victim which He truly sought, which He had in mind for Himself. This is the victim,[1] dedicated with our whole heart, fed on faith, cared for with truth, unblemished in innocence, clean in purity, an offering of love garlanded, that we ought to escort to God's altar, in company with a procession of good works, 'midst psalms and hymns, and it will obtain all things for us from God.

29. What will God refuse to prayer that comes from

---

[1] See note 2, p. 34.

spirit and truth, since such He demands? We read and hear and see how great are the proofs of His power. Even the prayer of the olden times freed men from fire and wild beasts and starvation, and yet it had not received its pattern from Christ. But how much more does Christian prayer work! It does not plant the angel of moisture "in the midst of a fire" or "stop the mouths of lions" or bring country fare to the starving; it turns away no feeling of suffering by the gift of grace, but furnishes sufferers and the victims of intense feeling and pain, with the power to endure; it extends grace to include courage, that faith may know what it is to get from the Lord, realising what it is suffering for God's name. But even in past days prayer inflicted scourges, routed the hosts of the enemy, stayed the benefit of rain showers. Now, however, righteous prayer turns away all the wrath of God, keeps watch in face of the enemy, "begs for the persecutors." Is there any wonder that it can wring water from the sky, seeing that it could obtain even fire? Prayer is the only thing that can prevail with God, but Christ willed that it should work no evil. All the power He conferred upon it sprang from good. So it has no power except to recall the souls of the dead from the very way of death, to restore the maimed, to cure the sick, to purge the victims of evil spirits, to open the bars of the prison, to loosen the bonds of the upright. It also washes away sins, drives back temptations, quenches persecutions, consoles the downhearted, cheers the courageous, attends upon the traveller in distant lands, subdues waves, confounds robbers, nourishes the poor, guides the rich, raises the fallen, supports the falling, and upholds them that do stand. Prayer is a wall for faith, a shield and a weapon

cf. Dan. iii. 92, 93; vi. 22, 23 1 Kings xvii. 15 cf. Dan. iii. 92 cf. Heb. xi. 33

cf. Exod. vii., etc. Exod. xvii. 13 Deut. xi. 17 cf. Matt. v. 44

against the enemy who watches us from all sides. Therefore let us never go forth unarmed. Let us bethink ourselves of the station by day, and of watching by night. Under the armour of prayer let us guard the standard of our commander, let us in prayer await the angel's trump. All the angels likewise pray, and every creature, beasts of the field and wild beasts pray and bend the knee, and as they leave the stable or the cave, look up to heaven with no vain utterance, stirring their breath after their own manner. Even the birds as they rise in the morning, wing their way up to heaven, and make an outstretched cross with their wings in place of hands, and utter something that seems a prayer. What more, then, is there to say on the duty of prayer? Even cf. Matt. the Lord Himself prayed, to whom be honour and xiv. 23, etc. power for ever and ever.

CONCERNING BAPTISM

1. HAPPY mystery of our water, because the sins of
our former blindness are washed away and we are freed
for everlasting life! The present treatise will not be
useless, if it instruct alike those who are at this moment
being formed, and those who, satisfied with simple belief,
do not investigate the grounds of what has been handed
down, and in inexperience carry an untried credible
faith. And further, a certain viper of the Gaian per-
suasion,[1] who lived here recently, has carried away very
many with her poisonous teaching, which aimed particularly at the abolition of Baptism. In this she clearly
acted according to nature: for it is the habit of vipers
and asps and even basilisks to haunt dry and waterless
spots. But we little fish, like our Fish Jesus Christ,[2] are
born in water, and it is only by remaining in water that
we are safe. Therefore that monster, who even in her
days of innocence was without the right to teach, well
knew how to slay the little fish by removing them from
the water.

2. Yet so great is the power of frowardness for the
undermining or the entire rejection of faith, that it

cf. 1 Tim,
ii. 12

[1] See the Introduction.

[2] The first letters of the five words, "Jesus Christ, of God Son,
Saviour," in Greek, spell the common noun meaning "a fish."
This gave rise to the use of the latter word as an emblem of Christ
and Christianity, and to various fanciful views hence derived.

employs the materials of which it consists as a ground of attack upon it! There is really nothing that so blinds men's minds as the simplicity of divine works seen in process and their grandeur promised in the result: for example in this connexion also, since with so great simplicity, without any parade or novel equipment, without any expense even, a man is lowered into water and with intervals for a few words is dipped, and rises up again not much cleaner or even no cleaner, and yet an incredible result in eternity is deemed to be assured. I am mistaken, if the appointed ritual or hidden mysteries of idol-worship do not, on the contrary, build up for themselves the belief and influence they have, from the splendour[1] and cost of their elaborate preparations. Piteous unbelief, which deniest to God His own special qualities, simplicity and power! What then? is it not wonderful that even death can be washed away by a bath?[2] And indeed this is all the more to be believed, if it is not believed for the reason that it is wonderful. For what character suits the divine works except one beyond all admiration? We ourselves also are full of wonder, but it is because we believe. Unbelief, however, wonders but believes not. It wonders at simple things, looking on them as useless, at extraordinary things as being impossible. By all means let it be as you suppose; but a divine pronouncement is quite ready with an

---

[1] Thus do I render *suggestu* in accordance with the view of Prof. August Engelbrecht of Vienna, who gives the best account of this difficult word, in *Wiener Studien*, Bd. XXVIII. (1906), pp. 9–17. It is here almost synonymous with *apparatus, ornatus, cultus, habitus, pompa.*

[2] I have throughout translated *lauacrum* by "bath," *tinguere* by "dip"; but no doubt Tertullian uses them in the sense "baptism," "baptize." The latter is indeed the older Latin word in this sense, and prevails in Tertullian. Very soon it had to give place to *baptizare*, and it is comparatively little found in later authors.

1 Cor. i.
27

answer to both attitudes "God chose the foolish things of the world to confound its wisdom," and what is excessively difficult to man is easy to God. For if God is both wise and powerful—and this is not denied even by those that neglect Him—He did right to place the materials of His working in the opponents of wisdom and power, namely in foolishness and powerlessness; since all strength gets its motive power from those by whom it is called forth.

3. While keeping in mind this pronouncement as a kind of regulation, we nevertheless consider how foolish and impossible it is that restoration should come by water, and why in any case this material has earned a function so worthy. In my opinion the authority belonging to the liquid element requires examination. As a matter of fact it is amply attested, and indeed from the beginning. For it is one of those elements which, before the world was created at all, rested with God in Gen. i.
1, 2 a form as yet rude. "In the beginning," Scripture says, "God made heaven and earth. But the earth was invisible and in disorder, and there was darkness over the deep, and the spirit of the Lord moved over the waters." It is your duty, oh man, to hold in reverence, in the first place, the age of the waters, because their substance is ancient, in the second place their worth, as the home of the divine spirit, more pleasing assuredly than the other elements at that time. For darkness was as yet entirely shapeless, being without the ornament of the stars, and the deep was forbidding, the earth was unready and the sky was unformed; water alone, the ever perfect matter, joyous, simple, unmixed in its very essence, provided a worthy vehicle for God. Again, later, the arrangement of the world took form for God, the waters

somehow exercising a regulative function. For it was by "separating the waters" that He suspended "the firmament" of heaven "in the middle"; it was by placing the waters apart that He contrived to raise the dry land. Then, when the world had been arranged in elements and was receiving inhabitants, "the waters" first were commanded "to bring forth living beings." "Water" first "gave forth what was to live": do not then be surprised that in Baptism waters are able to give life. Was not, too, the work of shaping even man himself completed by the association of waters therewith? The substance was made up of earth, but earth is not manageable unless it be wet and juicy, and it the waters that had been moved away before the fourth day to their proper position had naturally, by reason of the moisture still remaining, modified to the consistency of mud. If I were to go on and detail all or many of the facts which I might mention about the importance of this element, how great its power is or the favour it confers, how many devices, how many functions, how great a power of work it brings to the world, I fear that I should be regarded as having gathered together the praises of water rather than the arguments for Baptism, even though I taught all the more fully the indisputable fact that God caused the matter, which He arranged in all His possessions and works, to carry out His will in His own mysteries also, that the matter which regulates the earthly life, acts as His agent in the heavenly also.

cf. Gen. i. 6, 7

cf. Gen. i. 20

cf. Gen. ii. 7

4. But it will be enough at the outset to seize upon those features in which the essential character of Baptism is recognised. Its first aspect is that by which even in those days the very attitude gave an early indication of the manner of Baptism, namely that "the spirit of God,"

D

cf. Gen. i.   which from the beginning "moved upon the" primal
2   "waters," would rest over the waters of Baptism. More-
              over, it was certainly a holy thing that moved over what
              was holy, and the supporting waters borrowed their
              holiness from that which moved over them.   Every
              underlying substance must catch the quality of that
              which is suspended over it, particularly when the former
              is corporeal and the latter is spiritual, as the spiritual
              by the fineness of its substance can easily penetrate the
              corporeal, and also settle in it.   So the nature of the
              waters, having been made holy from that which is holy,
              has itself also conceived the power to sanctify.   Let no
              one say: "Are we really dipped [1] in the very waters
              which existed then in the beginning?"   Not, of course,
              the very waters, except to the extent to which, while there
              is one class, there is a number of subdivisions.   What
              belongs to the class extends also to the subdivision.
              Therefore there is no difference whether one is washed
              in the sea or in a pool, in a river or in a spring, in a
              lake or in a river bed, and there is no difference between
cf. Matt.   those whom John "dipped in the Jordan" and Peter in
iii. 6   the Tiber,[2] unless it be true also that the eunuch whom
cf. Acts
viii. 38   Philip baptized on his journey with such water as
              offered, obtained more, or less salvation than others.
              Therefore all waters by virtue of the old privilege
              belonging to their origin, obtain the mystery of sanctifi-
              cation after God has been invoked.   For immediately
              the Spirit comes from heaven over them, and is above
              the waters sanctifying them from itself, and being thus
              sanctified they imbibe the power of sanctifying.   And

---

[1] See note 2, p. 47.
[2] The tradition that St. Peter had lived and worked in Rome is
here assumed without question.

yet the parallel would accord with the simple act, namely that since we are stained by sins as if by filth, we may be washed by the waters. But although sins do not appear in the flesh (since no one bears on his skin the stain of idolatry or rape or fraud), yet their like are foul within the spirit, which is the originator of sin. For the spirit is lord, the flesh is its slave. Yet both share the guilt with one another, the spirit because of its command, the flesh because of its óbedient service. Therefore when the waters have been treated in a certain way by the intervention of the angel, the spirit is bodily washed in the waters and the flesh is spiritually cleansed in the same.

5. But you will tell me that peoples without the slightest understanding of spiritual things attribute power to their images of gods through the same efficacy in water. These, however, deceive themselves, since the water they use is bereft of spiritual power. For they are initiated into certain sacred rites by a bath, those of some [1] Isis or Mithras; even their very gods they exalt with washings. Indeed, it is a universal custom to carry water round estates, houses, temples and whole cities, for their purification by sprinkling. It is true that at the celebrations in honour of Apollo [2] and those held at Pelusium,[3] worshippers are dipped, and they have

---

[1] It is a favourite device of Tertullian to prefix " some " (*aliquis*) to a proper name, when he wishes to show his contempt for the person ; see the Index to Mayor's Tertullian *Apologeticus* for other instances. The Romans for long had been thoroughly familiar with the foreign cults here mentioned, that of Isis, the Egyptian goddess, and of Mithras, the Persian sun-god. The former worship appealed especially to women, the latter to men.

[2] The *Ludi Apollinares*, celebrated particularly at Rome.

[3] It is not quite certain what is intended by the reference to Pelusium (Sarapis ?). But it is far better criticism to retain *Pelusiis*, confessing our ignorance, than to alter to *Eleusiniis*, which being generally understood, would never have been corrupted by any

the effrontery to declare that their object is rebirth and an escape from punishment for their broken oaths. Likewise among the men of old, whoever had stained himself with homicide, sought out waters of cleansing power. Therefore, if from their nature in itself, because they are the appropriate means of cleansing, waters charm such devotees by giving good promise of purification, how much more truly will waters confer that benefit through God's authority, by Whom all their nature has been established ! If they think water is given a special property by religion, what better religion is there than that of the living God ? When He is recognised, here also we perceive the zeal of the devil in seeking to rival the things of God, since he too practises a baptism among his followers. What likeness is there ? The unclean cleanses, the destroyer frees, the condemned acquits. It is plain that it is his own work he will be undoing if he washes away sins inspired by himself. These remarks, of course, are set down as evidence against those who reject the faith, if they do not believe the things of God, while believing the imitations of these furnished by God's enemy. Do not unclean spirits also at other times, without any mystery, brood over the waters, counterfeiting that movement of cf. Gen. i. the divine spirit at the beginning ? This is known to
2 all springs in dark places, all remote streams, pools in the baths, channels in houses or cisterns and wells, which are said to carry people off, of course by the power of a malignant spirit. For they call those by the names [1] . . . and lymphatic (*lit.* affected by water) and

---

scribe to *Pelusiis*. Tertullian is our only authority for other features of Pagan religion also.

[1] The MS. read apparently *et esietos* or *esietos*, which letters must

hydrophobic (*lit.* afraid of water), those whom waters have choked (drowned) or afflicted with madness or terror.   To what purpose have we recalled these beliefs? Lest any one should think it too difficult that a holy angel of God should be present at the adaptation of the waters for the salvation of a man, when an evil angel is accustomed to engage in profane intercourse with the same element for the destruction of a man. If it seems an unheard-of thing that an angel should interfere with water, there was a precedent for that which was to be.   The pool of Bethsaida "was stirred" by the intervention of "an angel."[1]   Those who complained of their health, used to watch for him.   For any one who had first descended there, ceased to complain after a bath.   This picture of bodily cure was prophetic of spiritual cure, according to the practice by which things carnal always precede, being a picture of things spiritual.   As, therefore, the grace of God spread among men, greater power was added to the waters and the angel.   Those who healed bodily defects, now heal the spirit; those who worked temporal salvation, now restore for us everlasting salvation; those who freed one once a year,[2] now daily save communities, death being destroyed by the washing away of sins.   With the removal of guilt there goes, of course, the removal of

cf. John v. 4

---

conceal some word meaning "water," or "drowned."   Perhaps Gelenius' *enectos* is right, but more probably some Græco-Latin word is latent.

[1] Tertullian is our earliest dateable authority for this verse, now regarded as an interpolation.   See the R.V. margin, and find the authorities for and against the interpolation in my edition of the Revisers' Text *ad. loc.*

[2] Tertullian therefore interprets the words *kata kairon* (John v. 4, R.V. marg., "at certain seasons") as meaning "once a year." Latin MSS. that do not shirk the phrase altogether, render by *cata* (*secundum, per*) *tempus.*

punishment also. So man, who had in the past been made "in the image of God," will be restored to God "in His likeness." "The image" is considered to be in the outward presentment, "the likeness" in eternity. For he recovers the spirit of God, which he had at that time received when breathed upon by Him, but had afterwards lost through sin.

6. I do not mean to say that we obtain the Holy Spirit in the water, but having been cleansed in the water, we are being prepared under the angel for the Holy Spirit. Here, also, a type preceded; for in the same way John was forerunner [1] of the Lord, "preparing His ways." So, also, the angel, the intermediary in Baptism, "makes straight the paths" for the Holy Spirit that is to come upon us, by the washing away of sins, obtained by faith that has been sealed in Father, Son and Holy Spirit. For if "on the word of three witnesses every word shall be established," how much more, while we have through blessing the same mediators of faith as we have guarantors of salvation, is the number of divine names sufficient for the confidence we feel in our hope! But although it is on the word of three that the witness to our faith and the covenant of our salvation alike are pledged, mention of the Church is added of necessity, since "where there are three," that is Father, Son and Holy Spirit, "*there*" is the Church, which is a body of three.

Gen. i. 26

cf. Matt. iii. 3, etc.
cf. Matt. iii. 3, etc.

Deut. xix. 15, etc.

cf. Matt. xviii. 20
cf. I John v. 7, 8

---

[1] Neither *antepræcursor* nor *ante præcursor* can be right. I believe Tertullian wrote *antecursor* (as in *Resurr.* 22, and in *Monog.* 8, *adv. Marc.* iv. 33, where it is used of John) here and in c. 11, and that a scribe, to whom the word was unfamiliar, corrected it in both places to the better known *præcursor*, with the result that in the MS. both prefixes were preserved.

7. Then, leaving the bath we are anointed all over[1] with blessed unction according to the primitive practice by which priests were wont to be anointed with olive oil from a horn. This custom obtained ever since Aaron was anointed by Moses, whence he is called "anointed" from the chrism, which is anointing. This adapted the name to the Lord, when it became spiritual. For He was anointed with the spirit by God the Father, as is stated in Acts: "For they were really gathered together in this city against Thy holy Son, whom Thou didst anoint." So also in us the anointing takes its course in a material sense, but it confers spiritual benefit, just as also the material act of Baptism itself, the fact that we are sunk in the water, becomes spiritual, in that we are freed from our sins.

cf. 1 Sam. xvi. 13

cf. Exod. xxx. 30 Lev. viii. 12, etc. cf. Matt. i. 16, etc. Acts iv. 27

8. Thereafter, a hand is laid on us by way of blessing, summoning and inviting the Holy Spirit. Human device will, of course, be permitted to summon air to water,[2] and to enliven their corporal union, by applying the hands above, with another blast of such distinctness; and will God not be allowed in the case of His own instrument to strike the note of spiritual elevation by means of holy hands? But this, too, comes from the old mystic rite by which Jacob blessed his grandsons, namely the sons of Joseph, Ephraim and Manasseh,

cf. Gen. xlviii. 14

---

[1] The force of the *per* in *perungimur* is somewhat doubtful, seeing that the anointing was confined to the forehead.

[2] The reference here is to the ancient water organ, invented by Ctesibius of Alexandria (cf. Plin. H. N. VII. § 125), and very popular in Rome in Nero's time. It played then a part like that of the wonderful creations of Gavioli and Marenghi in modern times. For details of the construction of the water organ consult Lupton's note on this passage, with his diagram, also Köstlin in Herzog-Hauck's *Real-Encyclopædie* and Kraus in *R. E. der christl. Altert.* II. pp. 557 f.

placing his hands on their heads, but interchanged, and indeed so transversely slanted, that representing Christ[1] they even then foretold the blessing that would be in Christ. Then that most holy spirit joyfully descends from the Father on cleansed and blessed bodies, and hovers over the waters of Baptism, as if recognising its ancient resting-place, "gliding down upon the Lord in the form of a dove," so that the nature of holy spirit was clearly shown by means of an animal of simplicity and innocence, for even in a physical sense the dove is without gall.[2] Therefore he says: "Be simple as doves"; this also contains an indication of the preceding type. For, as after the waters of the Flood, by which the sin of the old days was cleansed, after the baptism, if I may style it so, of the world, the dove as herald proclaimed to the earth peace from heaven's wrath, having been let go from the ark and having returned with the olive-branch—a token which is held out even among the heathen as harbinger of peace; by the same arrangement of a spiritual result there flies to the earth, that is our flesh, as it emerges from the bath after old sins are washed away, the dove of the Holy Spirit, bringing God's peace, having been sent out from heaven, where the Church is, that was represented by the ark. But the world sinned again; thus the comparison of Baptism to the Flood is a bad one. Therefore, the world is reserved for fire like the man who after Baptism engages again in sin, so that this, too, ought to be taken as a sign of warning to us.

9. How many protections, therefore, in nature, how

---

[1] They represent Christ because the first letter of *Christus* in Greek and Latin is X.

[2] This ancient belief is untrue to fact.

many privileges in grace, how many rites in outward religion, patterns, preparations, supplications, have regulated the worship connected with water! At first, for example, when the people, freed from the shackles of Egyptian bondage, escaped the violence of the king of Egypt by crossing the water, the water put an end to the king himself with all his forces. What pattern could be clearer in the mystery of Baptism! The nations are freed from the present world by water assuredly, and they leave behind them the devil, their former tyrant, overwhelmed in the water. Likewise the water is cured of the bitterness which spoilt it, and made sweet, useful and beneficial by Moses' rod. That wood was Christ, bringing healing, of course, out of Himself, to the streams of a nature that had once been poisoned and bitter, in the health-giving waters of Baptism. This is the water which flowed down for the people from "the attendant rock." For if "the rock is Christ," without doubt we see that Baptism is blessed by water in Christ. How great is the grace in water, where God and His anointed are present, for the ratification of Baptism! Christ is never apart from water: for even He Himself is baptized with water; when invited to a wedding He inaugurates with water the earliest trials of His power; when He speaks he invites them "that thirst" to His "everlasting water"; when He teaches about love, He commends the offering of "a cup of water" to a destitute person among the works of love; at a well He recovers His strength, "on water He walks," He crosses the water with delight, with water He serves His disciples.[1] The evidence of Baptism continues right to the time of His passion; when He is given over to the cross, water

cf. Exod. xiv. 28

1 Cor. x. 4

cf. Matt. iii. 16, etc.

cf. John ii. 7–9

cf. John iv. 14

cf. Matt. x. 42, etc.

cf. John iv. 6 ff.

cf. Matt. xiv. 25

cf. Matt. xiv. 34

cf. John xiii. 5

---

[1] Reading *aqua* (ablative case).

cf. Matt. xxvii. 24, etc.

interposes; Pilate's hands know this; when He is wounded, water breaks forth from His side; the soldier's spear knows it.

cf. Matt. xxvii. 49; John xix. 34

10. We have spoken, as far as our humble ability permitted, about all those elements which build up the religion of Baptism; now I will proceed as well as I am able to consider the rest of its constitution, with reference to certain minor questions. Baptism as proclaimed by John involved even at that time a question, put before the Pharisees even by the Lord Himself, namely, whether that Baptism was heavenly or really earthly. On this

cf. Mark xi. 30, etc.

cf. Mark xi. 33, etc.

matter they were unable to give a courageous answer, since they did not understand, for the reason that they

cf. Isa. vii. 9 (LXX)

did not believe either.[1] We, however, with understanding as meagre as is our faith, can express the opinion

cf. Mark xi. 30, etc.

that His baptism was indeed from heaven, divine in commission, however, not in power, because we read

cf. Luke iii. 2, etc.

that John also was sent by the Lord to perform this duty, but was merely human in his nature. For he

cf. Matt. iii. 3, etc.
cf. Matt. iii. 8, etc.

offered nothing heavenly, but he paved the way for the service of heavenly things, being, of course, given charge of penitence, which is in man's power. Indeed the doctors of the law and the Pharisees, who refused to

cf. Matt. xi. 20

believe, did not repent either. But if repentance is a human affair, Baptism must be of that very same nature; for if it had been heavenly, it would have conferred both the Holy Spirit and remission of sins.

---

[1] Here there is an allusion to a verse much quoted by the Fathers according to the Septuagint rendering, followed by the Old-Latin, which is : "And if ye do not believe, ye shall not understand either." The LXX is a translation of another Hebrew word like the true text (see Dr. G. Buchanan Gray's note *ad. loc.*, p. 120 of Vol. I. of his commentary on the *Book of Isaiah* in the International Critical Commentary). The true text in the Hebrew means, "If ye believe not, ye shall not be established" (Gray, p. 119, cf. R.V.).

But neither is sin forgiven nor the Spirit granted by any cf. Luke
one save God alone.   Even the Lord Himself said that v. 21
cf. John
"except He first ascended to the Father, the Spirit would xvi. 7
not descend."   What the Lord could not yet confer,
assuredly His slave would have been unable to offer.
Further, we find afterwards in the Acts of the Apostles
that those who had "the Baptism of John," had not cf. Acts
"received the Holy Spirit," whom "they did not know xviii. 25;
xix. 2
even by hearsay."   Therefore that was not heavenly
which did not show heavenly qualities, since the very
quality in John that had been heavenly, namely, the
spirit of prophecy, after the transference of the whole
spirit to the Lord, so failed that he afterwards sent men cf. Matt.
to ask whether He whom he had preached and whose xi. 3, etc.
arrival he had signalised, were really He.   It was, therefore, "a Baptism of repentance" that was carried on, as Mark i. 4,
a sort of candidate for the remission and sanctification etc.
that were soon to follow in Christ.   For "the Baptism of Mark. i. 4
repentance for the remission of sins" which he preached,
was announced with a view to the remission that was to
be; for penitence comes first, remission follows after, and
this is to prepare the way; he, however, who prepares, cf. Mark
does not himself complete, but sees to the completion at i.2; Matt.
iii. 3, etc.
the hands of another.   He himself declares that heavenly
things are not his, but the Christ's, when he says: "He John iii.
that is of the earth, speaketh the things of the earth; 31
but He who cometh from above is over all": also that
he baptized with a view to repentance only, while there
"would afterwards come one who would baptize in spirit cf. Luke
and fire."[1]   And this he said assuredly because a true iii. 16

---

[1] This interesting form of the text of Luke iii. 16 is supported
by Clement of Alexandria, *Eclog.* 25, and Augustine, *De Cons.
Evang.* II. 12 § 26 (see H. J. Vogels' tractate on the latter in
Biblische Studien, Bd. XIII. (1908) (5), pp. 35 f.).

and abiding faith is baptized with water for salvation, but a pretended and weak faith is baptized with fire for judgment.

11. "But behold," they say, "the Lord came and did not baptize." For we read : " And yet He did not baptize, but His disciples." As if John had proclaimed that He himself would actually baptize with His own hands ! It is not, of course, to be so understood, but as having been said simply in the ordinary way, as for example we say : "The emperor published an edict," or "the prefect lashed him with rods " :[1] does he himself publish, or he himself lay on the lash? He on whose behalf service is performed is always spoken of as acting. So the words " He himself will baptize you " must be taken as equivalent to "You will be baptized through Him or into Him." But let no one be troubled because He did not Himself baptize. For unto whom or what would He have baptized ? Unto repentance? What need, then, of a forerunner? Unto remission of sins, which He offered by a word? Unto Himself, whom in humility He concealed ? Unto the Holy Spirit, though He himself " had not yet ascended to His Father "? Into the Church, which the apostles had not yet built? Therefore His disciples baptized as His servants, as his forerunner John before Him, with the same baptism as John's, lest any one should suppose it was with a different Baptism : for there is no other except that later Baptism of Christ's, which could not, of course, be conferred at that time by the disciples. For the Lord's glory was not yet fulfilled, and the

---

[1] Illustrations derived from the emperor and magistrates are a feature of Ambrosiaster (*Study of Ambrosiaster*, pp. 23 ff.), but are not unknown to other writers, *e. g.* the "Clementine" books, and Ambrose, *In Psalm*, i. § 13 (ed. Bened. Ven. tom. II. p. 8. D.E.) ; *In Psalm*, cxviii. 10, § 25, 4.

efficacy of Baptism was not yet prepared by the passion and resurrection. Moreover, neither could our death be annulled except by the Lord's passion, nor could our life be restored without His resurrection.

12. When, then, the rule is laid down that salvation belongs to no one without Baptism, especially in accordance with the declaration of the Lord, who says : "Except one be born of water, he hath not life," there arise hesitant or rather reckless questionings on the part of some, how, if this rule is to hold, salvation can belong to the apostles, seeing we do not find that any of them were baptized in the Lord save Paul. Nay, more, seeing that Paul was the only one among them who experienced the baptism of Christ, they wonder whether the peril of the others who are without the water of Christ, is a foregone conclusion, if the rule be held inviolate, or whether the rule is repealed, if salvation has been settled even for those that have not been baptized. I have heard such words to which the Lord witnessed, lest any one should think me so reprobate as to go out of my way to use an author's fancy to devise what will inspire others with doubts. And now I will answer to the best of my power those who deny that the apostles were baptized. For if they had experienced the human baptism of John and went without the Lord's, because the Lord Himself had fixed Baptism as one, when he said to Peter who wished to be completely bathed : "He that hath washed once, hath no need to do so again" (which certainly he would not at all have said to an unbaptized person), this also is a clear proof against those who seek to deprive the apostles of John's baptism also, in order to destroy the mystery of water. Can it be thought credible that

cf. John iii. 5, vi. 47, etc.

cf. Acts ix. 18

John xiii. 10

cf. Matt.
iii. 3, etc. "the way of the Lord was" not then "prepared," namely, the baptism of John, in those persons who were destined to open up the Lord's way throughout the whole world? The Lord Himself, though in no way bound to show penitence, was baptized; was it not necessary for sinners? While it is true, then, that others were not baptized, still they were not followers of Christ, but enemies of the faith, teachers of the law and Pharisees. Thus, too, it is suggested that when the Lord's enemies refused to be baptized, those who followed the Lord had been baptized and had not shared "the wisdom" of their enemies. The Lord, on whom they were in constant attendance, had of course extolled John in the following words of commend-

Matt. xi.
11 ation: "No one is greater among them that are born of women, than John the Baptizer." Others by an interpretation that is clearly rather forced, insinuate that the apostles had fulfilled the duty of Baptism on the

cf. Matt.
viii. 24,
etc. occasion when they were sprinkled and overwhelmed by the waves in the boat; and that even Peter himself

cf. Matt.
xiv. 29 by stepping over the sea had been sufficiently immersed. In my opinion, however, it is one thing to be sprinkled or cut off by the sea's violence, another thing to be baptized by an ordinance of religion. But that boat represented a type of the Church, because on the sea, which is this present world, it is disturbed by waves— that is, persecutions and trials, while the Lord in His

cf. Matt.
viii. 24 forbearance "is" as it were "asleep," until by the prayers of saints He is at last aroused, puts restraint upon the world and restores calm to His own. But whether they were in some way or other baptized or

cf. John
xiii. 10 continued unwashed, so that the saying of the Lord also about one bath should, in the person of Peter, have reference to us only, it is, however, at present rather rash to pronounce an opinion on the salvation of the apostles, because a short way to Baptism could have been conferred upon them even by the privilege of their original promotion and their subsequent inseparable association with the Lord, since they, I believe, were following Him who promised salvation to every one that believed. "Thy faith," he used to say, "hath saved thee," and, "Thy sins will be forgiven thee," as be-lieving of course, but not, however, baptized. If the apostles were without that, I do not know by what faith, at one word from the Lord, a man arose and quitted the custom-house, another abandoned father and ship and the trade by which he made his livelihood, another disdained to attend his father's funeral, and obeyed before he had heard it, that supreme command of the Lord: "He that preferreth his father or mother to Me, is not worthy of Me."

Matt. ix. 22, etc.
Matt. ix. 2, etc.

cf. Matt. ix. 9, etc.
cf. Matt. iv. 20, etc.
cf. Matt. viii. 22, etc.
Matt. x. 37

13. It is in this connexion, then, that those criminals stir up questions. They actually say: "Baptism is not necessary to those for whom faith is enough; for Abraham also pleased God by no mystery of water, but by that of faith only." But in everything later practice settles a question, and what follows prevails over what has gone before. Let us admit that salvation came about in past times by simple faith, before the Lord's passion and resurrection; but when faith was increased (I mean by faith the belief in His nativity, passion and resurrection), there was added to the mystery, thus enlarged in scope,[1] a ratification in Baptism, in some

---

[1] I read here with Jülicher (*Theologische Litteraturzeitung* for 1909, p. 293) *ampliato* instead of *ampliatio*, and withdraw the comma after *sacramento*.

way a garment of faith, which previously was simple and now has no efficacy without obedience to its law. For the law of Baptism was enjoined and its ritual prescribed. "Go," he says, "teach the nations, baptizing them in the name of Father and Son and Holy Spirit." The addition to this law of the regulation: "Except one be born again of water and spirit, he shall not enter into the kingdom of heaven," bound faith to the necessity of Baptism. Consequently from that time all believers were baptized. Then Paul, also, when he believed, was baptized. And this is what the Lord also, in inflicting the scourge of blindness, had enjoined, saying: "Rise up, and enter Damascus; there you will be shown what you ought to do"; namely, to be baptized, the only qualification that was wanting to him. Apart from that he had sufficiently learnt and believed that "the Nazarene" was the Lord, the Son of God.

14. But with regard to the Apostle himself they raise the objection that he said: "For the Lord did not send me to baptize." (As if by this argument Baptism were abolished! For why did he baptize Gaius and Crispus and the house of Stephanas?) And yet, although Christ had not sent him to baptize, he had nevertheless taught the other apostles to baptize. But these were written to the Corinthians in view of the circumstances at that time, since cleavages and disagreements were stirring among them, while one gave the chief place to Paul and another to Apollos. On this account the peace-loving Apostle, lest he should be thought to claim everything for himself, said that he was sent not to baptize, but to preach. Besides, preaching comes first, Baptism later; and preaching did take place first. I fancy,

however, that he who was allowed to preach, was also
allowed to baptize.

15. I know not whether anything else is canvassed in
the dispute about Baptism. I will, of course, take up
what I have omitted above, lest I should be thought to
cut short the thoughts that are impending. There is for
us "one Baptism" only, of which we learn alike from
the Gospel of the Lord and from the letter(s) of the
Apostle, who says that there is "one God" and "one
baptism" and one Church in heaven. But one may
rightly consider, I admit, what course must be maintained
with regard to heretics. For it was to *us* that it was
proclaimed : but heretics have no share in our rule of
life ;[1] the very deprivation of intercourse testifies that
they are undoubtedly strangers. I am not bound to
recognise in them what has been enjoined on me,
because we have not the same god as they, nor have we
one Christ—I mean the same, and therefore we have not
one Baptism either, because it is not the same ; if they
have not Baptism as it should be, they are undoubtedly
without it, and it is not allowable that what they have
not should be counted ; so also they cannot receive it
either, because they have it not. But this matter I have
dealt with already at greater fullness in the Greek. Once
and once only, therefore, we enter the bath, once for all
are sins washed away, because they must not be repeated.
But the Jewish Israel washes daily, because he is daily
soiled. That this might not be the practice in our case
also, is the reason why a regulation was made about one
bath. Happy water, which once for all cleanses, which
is not a sport for sinners, which not being stained

cf. Eph.
iv. 5
cf. Matt.
xxviii. 9
cf. Eph.
iv. 5

---

[1] On this passage, see C. H. Turner in Swete, *Early History of
the Church and Ministry*, p. 152.

E

by continual experience of filth, does not stain again those whom it washes!

16. We have indeed a second bath too, which itself also is one, namely that of blood, about which the Lord says: "I have a baptism to be baptized with," although he had been already baptized. For "He had come through water and blood," as John wrote, that He might be baptized with water, and glorified by His shed blood, and might cause us likewise to be "called" by water, "chosen" by blood. Those two baptisms he sent forth from the wound of His pierced side, in order that those who believed in His blood might be washed with water, and those who had washed with water might also carry the stain of blood. This is the Baptism which makes real even a baptism that has not been received, and restores one that has been lost.

17. To bring our slight treatment of the subject to an end,[1] it remains to give hints also about the course to be followed in conferring and receiving Baptism. The highest priest, who is the bishop, has of course the right to confer it; then the presbyters and deacons, not, however, without the bishop's authority, out of respect to the Church: when this respect is maintained, peace is secure. But besides, even laymen have the right to baptize; for that which is received alike by all, can be by all alike conferred; unless you argue that the name "disciples" belongs only to bishops or presbyters or deacons. The Word of the Lord ought not to be hidden from any one. In like manner Baptism also, which is equally a divine institution, can be practised by all. But how much more is the practice of modesty and

---

[1] On this chapter consult F. E. Brightman in Swete, *Early History of the Church and Ministry*, pp. 390 ff.

obedience binding upon laymen, since those privileges are suited to their superiors, lest they should assume the duty that is assigned to bishops! Hostility to the bishop's position begets schisms. The most holy Apostle said that "all things were permissible, but that all things were not expedient." Let it suffice certainly to take advantage of the privilege in cases of necessity, if anywhere the circumstances either of the place or the time or the person compel it. For then is the boldness of the helper welcomed, when the situation of the endangered person is pressing, since he will be guilty of ruining a human being if he refrains from offering what he was freely able to confer. But the forwardness of a woman who has presumed to teach will not of course acquire for her the right of baptizing also, unless some new beast appear like unto the old, so that just as that one took away Baptism, so some beast should by herself confer it. But if they claim writings which are wrongly inscribed with Paul's name [1]—I mean the example of

---

[1] Tertullian alone records for us the circumstances of the composition of "The Acts of Paul," the original form of which exists only in a (fragmentary) Coptic translation. The work was composed in Greek, possibly at Smyrna, about A.D. 160, and was translated into Latin as well as into Coptic, etc, The book was produced with a worthy enough motive, being based in the main on the canonical Acts of the Apostles. The part of the narrative dealing with Thecla was largely circulated by itself, and survives in numerous copies. She was reported to be a convert of St. Paul, belonging to the district of Iconium and Pisidian Antioch, and "became the type of the female Christian teacher, preacher, and baptizer" (Ramsay, *Church in the Roman Empire*, p. 375; his Chap. XVI. is a searching examination of the historical character of the story). See Carl Schmidt, *Acta Pauli. Uebersetzung, Untersuchungen und koptischer Text*, 2te Ausg. (Leipzig, 1905), Oskar v. Gebhardt, *Passio S. Theclæ Virginis: Die latein. Uebersetzgn. der Acta Pauli et Theclæ nebst Fragm., Auszügen u. Beilagen* (Leipzig, 1902), E. Hennecke, *Neutestamentliche Apokryphen* (Tübingen, 1904), *Handbuch zu den Neutestamentlichen Apokryphen* (Tübingen, 1905), and for the supposititious Pauline correspondence with Corinth, which formed part

Thecla—in support of women's freedom to teach and baptize, let them know that a presbyter in Asia, who put together that book, heaping up a narrative as it were from his own materials under Paul's name, when after conviction he confessed that he had done it from love of Paul, resigned his position. For how consonant would it seem with faith that he should give woman the power to teach and baptize, who consistently refused permission to woman even to teach? "Let them keep silence," he says, "and ask their husbands' advice at home."

cf. 1 Cor. xiv. 34
1 Cor. xiv. 34

18. But that Baptism is not lightly to be conferred, is known to those whose duty it is to confer it. "Give thyself to every one that asketh" has likewise its own reason, which is bound up with almsgiving. Rather must one give close attention to that other passage: "Give not the holy thing to the dogs and cast not your pearl[1] before swine"; and: "Lay not on hands too readily, lest you share in another's sins." If Philip baptized the eunuch so readily, let us reflect that the clear and plain testimony of the Lord to his worthiness had intervened. The Spirit had commanded Philip to proceed along that "road"; the eunuch himself also was found not in idleness, not such a man as eagerly desired to be baptized on a sudden, but one who having set out for the temple "to pray," had his attention riveted on the divine Scripture. In such an attitude should he be surprised, to whom God had actually sent an apostle, whom again "the Spirit" commanded, this time "to join himself to the eunuch's chariot"; the passage of Scripture fitted to

Luke vi. 30

Matt. vii. 6

1 Tim. v. 22
cf. Acts viii. 38
cf. Acts viii. 6 ff.
cf. Acts viii. 26
cf. Acts viii. 27, 28

cf. Acts viii. 26
cf. Acts viii. 29

---

of the *Acta Pauli*, see A. v. Harnack in *Sitzungsberichte d. preuss. Akad.* for 1905, p. 3, and D. de Bruyne in *Revue Bénédictine* for 1908, pp. 431 ff.

[1] There seems to be no doubt that Tertullian read the singular here : I know no other authority for it.

inspire faith itself comes his way at the right time, the exhortation is accepted, the Lord is shown, faith delays not, there is no waiting for water, the Apostle, his task cf. Acts viii. 36 completed, "is snatched away." But even Paul was cf. Acts viii. 39 really baptized in a hurry: for Simon[1] his host had speedily learned that he was made "a chosen vessel." Acts ix. God's approval puts forward its own rights; every 15 request can both deceive and be deceived. Consequently in view of the circumstances and will, even the age of each person, a postponement of Baptism is most advantageous, particularly, however, in the case of children. For what need is there, if it is not so urgent, that the sponsors also should be brought into danger, being as they are themselves also by reason of their mortality capable of falling short of their promises and being deceived by the development of an evil disposition? The Lord indeed says: "Forbid them not to come unto Matt. xix. Me." Let them come, then, while they are growing up; 14 let them come while they are learning, while they are being taught whither to come; let them become Christians, when they have been able to know Christ. Why hurries the age of innocence to the remission of sins? Shall we act more cautiously in worldly matters? Shall one to whom earthly substance is not entrusted, be entrusted with heavenly? Let them know how to seek salvation, that you may be seen "to give to him that asketh." For cf. Matt. vii. 7, etc. no less reason the baptism of the unmarried also should be postponed, for in them a testing has been prepared alike for virgins through their maturity and for widows through their freedom from the duty of marriage, until they either marry or are hardened for the practice of continence. If any should understand the importance

---

[1] Tertullian's mistake for Ananias.

of Baptism, they will be more afraid of its consequences than of its postponement; unimpaired faith is sure of salvation.

19. Good Friday offers the more regular occasion for Baptism, when also the Lord's passion into which we are baptized was consummated. And it will not be interpreted inconsistently with the type that when the Lord was to celebrate His last passover, on sending His disciples to prepare, He said, "You will meet a man carrying water," and thus indicated the place for the celebration of the passover by the sign of water. Next, Whitsuntide is the most joyous period for the administration of Baptism, at which both the Lord's resurrection was widely made known among the disciples, and the gift of "the Holy Spirit" was inaugurated, and the hope of the Lord's advent suggested, when on His having then been "received back into the heavens," the angels said to the apostles that "He would come in the very way in which He ascended into heaven," namely at Whitsuntide. But indeed when Jeremiah says: "And I will gather them together from the farthest parts of the earth on a festal day," he indicates the day of Good Friday and of Whitsunday, which is properly "a festal day." However, every day is the Lord's, every hour, every time is suitable for Baptism: if there is a difference in regard to the proper season, there is none in regard to the grace.

20. Those about to enter on Baptism should supplicate with frequent prayers, fastings, genuflexions and vigils, and with confession of all their past sins, that they may set forth the baptism of John also: "they were baptized," we are told, "confessing their sins." We must be congratulated if we now in presence of the congregation confess our iniquities or meannesses. For we are at one

and the same time both making an apology for the past with a struggle between flesh and spirit, and raising up beforehand defences against the trials that are to follow. "Watch and pray," he says, "lest ye fall into a testing situation." And the reason, I believe, why they were tested was that they fell asleep, with the result that they failed the Lord after His arrest, and that he who continued with Him and made use of a sword, actually denied Him thrice; for the saying also had preceded, that no untried person would attain the heavenly realms.[1] The Lord Himself immediately after Baptism was beset by trials, "having fasted for forty days." "Therefore we also," some one will say, "ought rather to fast after Baptism." And who is to forbid us except the duty to rejoice and give thanks for our salvation? But the Lord, to the best of my humble belief, by following the pattern of Israel, cast back a reproach upon him. For the people, after crossing the sea and being brought thence into the desert, though fed there by supplies from God for forty years, remembered the belly and the palate as much as they did God. Afterwards the Lord, "having been moved away to desert places" after Baptism and "having made an end of forty days' fasting," showed that a "man" of God does "not live on bread, but by the Word of God," and that the trials associated with repletion and the excessive gratification of the belly, are crushed by abstinence. Therefore, ye blessed ones[2] on whom the grace of God waits, when ye come up from that most

cf. Eph. vi. 12

Matt. xxvi. 41, etc.

cf. Matt. xxvi. 40, etc.

cf. Matt. xxvi. 51, etc.

cf. Jas. i. 12, and see note.

cf. Matt. iv. 2, etc.

cf. Exod. xvi. 3

cf. Matt. iv. 1, etc.

cf. Matt. iv. 2, etc.

cf. Matt. iv. 4, etc.

---

[1] I am by no means certain that Resch (*Agrapha*[2], p. 130 = *Agraphon* 90 [L. 26]) is right in equating this quotation with a saying frequently found in Greek (especially Syrian) sources as from Scripture : "The man who has not been tried, is not approved [before God]." The trial has reference especially to faith.

[2] *i. e.* catechumens.

holy bath of new birth, and before your Mother [1] and with your brethren ye spread out your hands for the first time, ask of the Father, ask of the Lord that the gifts of grace, "the partitions" of spiritual endowments be added thereto. "Ask and ye shall receive," He says. Ye have indeed asked and found ; ye have knocked and the door has been opened unto you. I only pray that, when ye ask, ye may also remember Tertullian, a sinner.

cf. Heb.
ii. 4
Matt. vii.
7
cf. Matt.
vii. 7

[1] See p. 21, *n.* I.

INDEX OF SCRIPTURE AND
OTHER PASSAGES

www.ingramcontent.com/pod-product-compliance
Lightning Source LLC
Chambersburg PA
CBHW070734030726
47601CB00001B/14